EILEEN CASEY
Dublin County, is
Her poetry has won numerous awards, both national and international. She was shortlisted for a *Sunday Tribune* Hennessy Award in Emerging Poetry in 2004. She has shown three poetry installations: Seagulls (Tallaght Community Arts Centre, 2006), Reading Fire, Writing Flame (Áras an Chontae, Tullamore, Co. Offaly, 2007) and The Jane Austen Sewing Kit, which featured during Birr Vintage Week and Arts Festival, 2007. She received literature bursaries from South Dublin County Council in 2005 and 2008 and she was the recipient of the Tyrone Guthrie Award from Offaly County Council in 2006. She works as a Creative Writing Facilitator for Dublin County VEC, Old Bawn Community School, Tallaght, and is a part-time tutor with Kilroy's College, Home Tuitions. She is currently completing a BA (Humanities) with Oscail, DCU.

Acknowledgments

Eileen Casey's poetry has been published widely in literary journals, magazines and anthologies, including: *Ireland of the Welcomes, Books Ireland, Senior Times, The Offaly Anthology, County Lines, The Salmon* (Issue 20), *Samhlaíocht Chiarraí Podium V, Heart of Kerry, The Space We Share* (The Patrick Kavanagh Rural & Literary Resource Centre), *The 2005 Bealtaine Brochure* (Age & Opportunity, Marino Institute of Education), *Aids West, Women's Work*.

Acknowledgments are due to the editors of the following, where some of these poems first appeared: *Poetry Ireland, The Sunday Tribune, The Cúirt Journal, Dancing the Rainbow, Riposte, West 47, Making Shapes with Slate and Marla* (A Gurteen Anthology), *The Chaffin Journal* (USA), *The Coffee House* (UK). 'Home' is part of a larger work (*Black Ball Gown*), commissioned by Paris-based artists Anne Cleary and Denis Connolly for 'City Loops', InContext 3, South Dublin County Council.

Thanks also to the following: Tallaght Library, Birr Library, Offaly County Council, South Dublin County Council, Dermot Bolger, Margaret Hogan, Tallaght Community Arts Centre.

For Saoirse

Contents

- 1 Salvage
- 3 Absence of Ocean
- 4 Synesthesia Sat
- 6 Miracles
- 7 Black Ball Gown
- 9 The Redheaded Whore of the Sea
- 11 On the Burning of the Kirov Ballet Costumes
- 12 Waxing Lyrical
- 13 Them
- 14 Crow Memory
- 15 Seagulls
- 16 Reading Fire, Writing Flame
- 17 Crash
- 18 At This Table
- 19 Presence of Mind
- 20 The Lion Tamer and the Fisherman
- 22 First Love
- 23 To the Woman Who Walked the Belly of the Moon
- 25 Leviathan
- 27 My Dress Hangs There
- 28 Strawberry Thief
- 30 Mr Einstein
- 31 For Emily
- 32 Firebirds
- 34 Star-splitters
- 35 Vodka Light
- 36 Fire Fox
- 37 Kestrel at Tymon Park
- 39 The Man With Scythes for Arms
- 41 An Fear Gorm

42	Hummingbird and Owl
43	Photographs of a Girl
46	Novenas
47	Warriors
49	Woman in a White Headscarf
50	Gold
52	Cinema Paradiso
54	Song
56	Derelict
57	Crane
58	Man at Sea
59	Missing
60	Brown Bird Bottle
62	Wish

Salvage

A day the sky falls in
I pick up as much as I can carry,
spread it over formica, a kitchen table
at first light; write down all I remember,
how it happened, the gory bits.
When that's done, I put it on my bed for sheets,
tussle it damp from night sweats into dreams,
wear it out.

I write on the flat surfaces of stones, lift
each one so what's buried there crawls
across my fingers. I write on birds'
droppings; it tells me where they've been,
where they might be headed.

I write on the blank screens of windows.
On towels hung over apartment balconies.
I write two straight afternoons
on a woman's begging bowl, how her child
will soon be too big for a swaddling sling.

I write on the blood dripping from a prime cut
steak. On the long aisles in supermarkets;
the queue in the labour exchange, the backs
of heads blocking my view in cinemas.
I write on the razor thin edge of the moon

sling it back into space.

I write on the bare legs of my children.
I write the names of my children on potato skins
curling from my knife. I write on names

long gone from here. I write the names
on the dust of buildings long gone from here,

a day the sky falls in.

Absence of Ocean

There's the story of a woman who left the West
and married into the Midlands, who never
saw the sea again.

All those peat-baked summers,
bog instead of beach.

No sea-blues sea-greens seen
or songs to gather up
in singing shells.
No seagulls to drown out children
limpets on her sea-rock.

But the sea was in her voice.
Across a flat, unsalted landscape
its rise and fall was like

a smooth stone skimming.

Synesthesia Sat
(*Birr Union Workhouse Installation, August 2007*)

Heartbreak is a colour
bruised deep in hollowed stairways
leading to cavernous rooms.

Tears taste the words
Love will tear us apart
playing on a record that spins
in my head for months after

it is sung in this place
by the grandmother
of a woman I know.

Embedded in a ceiling,
star-paths map trails
on midnight roadsides;

sprinkling the sound of bone
on silvering bone.

Her hands held out in invitation,
a woman sits cross-legged
on bare boards.
I kneel, touch her warm flesh,
close my eyes
become
a bare foot
sinking into
skylark song,
a mouth

welled with silence,
ears seeing
what hungry eyes
could not.

I am a wheel
circling
skins of scattered stones,

all my senses
turning.

Miracles

When the stone stare fixed upon a fevered eye
pilgrims came to ferment faith with the fruit of Her
womb.

That sultry season they looked for signs,
hung garlands about the granite throat,
withered petals strewing away
all promise of spinning suns.

In August heat the fervour wilted;
they left that sacred place.

Blackberries that rosaried the hillside
untouched by reverent fingers
purple sluiced their burning bush

never to stain the pot,
be poured into jam wine.

Black Ball Gown

It's Wednesday, that in-between day.
I buy milk, bread, ham (enough for two)
and a black ball gown.

Black skirts billow swan feathers,
a black swan. Rare sighting among
old jumpers, reeds of windows' weeds
in the second-hand clothes shop.

Old shoes with loose tongues bring to mind
gossiping women in Mr. Bohannan's
(at least that's how the name sounded to a child)
sorting through the rubble of others' leavings,
searching out what was worth keeping,
the way Mr. Bohannan must have sorted
through the rubble of Europe.

I want to bury my head in its folds,
smell the smell of tulle.
I carry it back to the bed-sit
beyond Leonard's Corner. A stream of black
flows through my arms, through the mouth
of a paint peeling front door (No. 8)
up the stairs into the one room
where my sister and I sleep and cook and dream
(the ceiling has a black disc of smoke
we burn so many meals, smoke so many cigarettes).

My black ball gown hangs across the wardrobe
for the whole of the year
I stay in that flat. I am barely eighteen,
not wanting to leave the nest of my Midland home.

There is no work there and besides
I have learned to type and take shorthand.

I walk to work each day, down Clanbrassil Street
down the diving dip at Christ Church onto the quays;

screams of gulls skim beneath black cloud balloons
bounce off Liffey waters, summer smell of the river
wending me towards Heuston Station,

to the typing pool, no place for swans.

My black ball gown,
how it lifts those black balloons
softens black discs on smoky ceilings.

While my fingers stammer over the typewriter
strange Van Hool McArdle words
it keeps its shape, is always
exactly as I left it.

The Redheaded Whore of the Sea

Lapped and licked by water,
blood drips from her hair, shed
when mermen sliced into each other,
forgetting in the splurge and gasp of war
how to breathe properly.

Already her dampness stains earth.
Trees are naked here, stretching up limbs
in a dance that's going nowhere
to a sky that's seen it all;

until bold as brass onto the riverbank
she comes, heaving up what lies
in her belly. Hoping to net
some unsuspecting earth man,
claim solid ground
for her unborn son.

She is sick of hiding behind rocks,
of silvered salmon, men

who spawn and spawn again
while her minnows cannot swim
fast enough away from her.
Sick and tired of sunken eyes,
the madness of open seas
bucking into her.

Already her fish tail divides,
shaping skin and limb.

Gently she rocks
in the breeze that steadies her,
blows colour into her lips,
fondling nipples
that jut for an earthman
in the last catch of light.

On the Burning of the Kirov Ballet Costumes
(St. Petersburg, September 2003)

I imagine them lined up like carcasses,
row upon row of tulle
pale in the gauze of unbearable silence.

No one knows quite how it begins,
how firebirds with sequined eyes
curl from the melt of net,
leap through shattered glass
to lick red tongues
over an icy skyline.

Perhaps it is a careless flame,
thrown down
by watchman or wardrobe mistress,
ignites in sheaves of swan
feathering a sinewy dance
along folds of dry taffeta.
It might be
frictions too long confined
between hoop and bone,
flint into a flail of rhinestones
soaked in the heat
of an evening's performance.

Waxing Lyrical

A man with a fish-eye and a mouth full
of promises solid as icebergs,

looks down into the face of his future.

A woman whose nose is a bicycle pump
sniffing out gossip, blowing it up
out of all proportion.

Both man and woman,
well capable
of waxing lyrical,

map rhyming schemes
lovely as sonnets;

villan
elles.

Them

He has no mention of how the Africans
– especially the women –
walk with a sway to the hip, by Jesus,
that would knock the eye out of your head,
shame the best jivers in the place;

or how the multicoloured rig-outs they wear
light up jaded streets and, though
double dutch and ráiméis at the best of times,
the sounds they make have a rhythm to them
that would do the heart good,
and when all's said and done, wasn't it gas,
all the same,
how a man from as far beyond, it might be Timbuktu,
could have a mind for céilí music?

Nothing of the journey that brought them,
how it might have started like many another before
– and not too far from him either –
with the prick of a knife against the throat
or a belly swollen up from hunger.

Nothing, after spitting on the pavement,
except that a body couldn't get up or down the streets
without being blinded by the sight of them.

'It's like the Congo now' he says

'this poxy town'.

Crow Memory

Glutted on lemonade and cake,
the child was put to bed by a maiden aunt
who tucked her up with pecking mouth
in the under-wing of silences roosted
on the closing of a door;

the day powder flapped over flushed cheeks
in the mirror in the long hallway,
folded round the house
when her mother left
for the last time.

Seagulls

In the park near the Shopping Centre
a swell of seagulls makes an ocean
of morning skyline.
From hooded anoraks faces tilt upwards,
turtles startled from fleece-lined shells.

Women pushing toddlers up the steep hill
are circled by sirens
squawking over house alarms going off,
ambulances barely making corners.
A rise of gulls skims across cloud cauls,

drops down to land on curled grass.
Concrete and asphalt disappear
into pearl green foam, tiny pink tongues
spear discarded crumbs
through waves of wind.

Peaks of chill breezes balloon
this laundry of birds into flight. Remind me
it's washday, shirts and sailing sheets
feathering out on washing lines.

An African man walks towards me
black as a midnight sky.
He too is buffeted from home
as am I, come to think of it – though not as far.

The seagulls, this African man and me
here in this churning landscape
making what we can of it.

Reading Fire, Writing Flame

Often it was stepped into, that flame-hemmed dress.
Jezebel heat on silk burnt through sheerest

skin; dissolving into veins, out of which
was written whatever it was that helped
bear the pain of red.

Skeins of light skimmed in and out of
breathing. Flame licked over midnight miles,
lit only by dull stares at the bottoms of glasses
drained of every living drop.

Never enough to quench
those fires, never enough.

Barely enough to mount that horse
rode to hell and back.

Yet he made the journey,
whinnying breaths unsaddling
that flame-hemmed dress;

the stepping out
of its strange beauty.

Crash

When your photograph falls by accident
glass cracks open like broken headlights;
the windscreen shatters all over again.

Pinned under it
your face is slashed to pieces,
all those things I said to you

bleeding onto the floor.

I would pick out every shard
embedded in your hair,
drive each jagged word
back down midnight roads,
dim the oncoming glare from my eyes,
set you on

a starling's crowded highway switch-
                backing,
    knowing exactly where to fly;

have us walk free from this wreckage
with not one single scratch.

At This Table

We poured ourselves out in love or hate.
Homework done, we dealt cards
by flickering light of burning grate,
hands passing over deep etched scars.

Homework done, we dealt cards;
potatoes washed were thinly peeled,
hands passing over deep etched scars,
a slicing knife, a glint of steel.

Potatoes washed were thinly peeled.
Chickens gutted, stalks off cabbages cut,
a slicing knife, a glint of steel.
Learning to count. Mouths keeping shut.

Chickens gutted, stalks off cabbages cut,
patterns scored out for mending clothes.
Learning to count. Mouths keeping shut.
Needles and pins set in rows.

Patterns scored out for mending clothes,
schoolbooks and satchels, lessons learnt hard,
needles and pins set in rows.
Homework done, we dealt cards,

We poured ourselves out in love or hate
by flickering light of burning grate.

Presence of Mind

It is now known that a man who murdered two people,
left another barely breathing, went upstairs

to shave off the familiar before sleeping children
woke to their morning.

With hands that crushed hollows in a woman's throat
he lathered his face, began a ritual like any other man
on a day like any other.

Hands that shuddered steel into flesh,
cracked iron on bone,
crawled the blade over his own skin,
then rinsed clean.

As daylight dissolved traces of the night
he left; before sleeping children woke

to a world washed crimson.

The Lion Tamer and the Fisherman

Midsummer's the best time for carnival.
Hordes of young ladies, a lion tamer,
louts from the town kept in order, a fisherman's
catch, screaming girls netted in swing boats,
waists tiny, mouths showing slippery tongues,
a town upside down, a luminous moon.

Chair-o-planes chaining around the moon,
painted-on tigers, elephants, carnival
frenzies. Lions, knees, slippery tongues.
Spindles of sound rush out, lion tamer
looks up under thin skirts, girls in swing boats.
Hands in pockets, silver for the fisherman.

Stars spindle above steeple, fisherman
fishing for thrills is bulls-eyed by full moon
netting the screams of wriggling girls. Swing boats
high as mezzo sopranos, carnival
bravados spot-lit by the lion tamer.
Rain on tarpaulin is slippery as tongues.

Summer shoes in mud, slippery as tongues,
crawling things rise to surface, fisherman
weathering stickleback storms. The lion tamer
looks up. Girls let down ropes, like hair. Moon
is a tusk piercing stare onto carnival
blare. Squelches and squeals rise with swing boats.

No safety nets for drops from swing boats,
hands on the ropes are slippery as tongues
raw with the stain of summer carnival

frenzy. Wave after wave, poor fisherman
feeling the strain of such luminous moon.
Midnight darkens the gaze of the lion tamer.

The ruby red waistcoat of the lion tamer
makes garish those frocks of girls in swing boats
straining high with ropes towards luminous moon.
Midnight falls soft like a velvet tongue
slipping into facades, no escaping the fisherman.
Fish silver the green grass of carnival.

Midsummer's the best time for the lion tamer's net
Swing boats ballooning with the swell of the moon
A carnival of fisherman's slippery tongue.

First Love

To lift that latch
was like pulling back a trigger.
Breath held, downslide of steel
eased into clips of rain on galvanised roofs,
sucks of wind bloating mother's sheets.

Father's jacket, nest warm
hung on the outhouse door, a crumple
of plaid patterned wool.
I felt for shape
found slim white smoky fingers
swaddled by silver slips.

A captain sea-knotted my stomach,
'Players Please'
captioned under his smile.
His sea-blue eyes were deep as the distance
father kept from me,
his youngest, snail trailing across
afternoons he slept
before the night shift. I shook
like the thin white bones rattling
inside his box of matches,
struck in shadowed hollows of hands
cupped around pink lipped flames and whisky.

I lit that flicker
took the powdery taste of him
deep into my throat,
dizzy with love.

To the Woman Who Walked the Belly of the Moon

(For John)

It's 1982, the week of the big snow, remember?
You reel a little when you go outside to light a cigarette
so you feel blue light on your skin. It's still in the bones

two grown sons and two grown daughters later;
a grandchild coming in the summer.

Remember how you stirred its brightness
into cups of tea?

Heaped two spoons into your baby's formula
so he'd sleep the whole length of afternoon.

Still enough of it left to blanket grey rooftops
cover the railings, disappear concrete.

'Six degrees below freezing' your new husband says.
Under the kitchen's bare bulb
his hair, back then, is black as a seal come up from the ice.
He says, 'the North wind brought it'
but you don't care for that explanation do you?

Preferring to think helicopters in the night
drop emergency packages of moon.

You see tiny traces of crowfeet, hear wolves
howling around the houses.

On the third afternoon
you bundle yourself into cardigans and coat,
walk around and around the belly of track
your body warming like a furnace,
holding heat just long enough
to make tender those moments before dawn

and him getting up for work, hoping
the car will start and when it doesn't
coming back into the house for a warm kettle
a refill of moon.

On the seventh day that terrible sound
moon prairie trickling down the drains
a circle of tundra scarcely visible in the night sky

leaving such ache
you never forget.

Leviathan

(*Birr Castle Telescope and Gardens, 2007*)

November trees are constellations
mapping familiar paths through orchards
scenting back to earth.

I see myself, a swirl of a girl at twelve, run
wild with two brothers this long lens of avenue,
our limbs unfolding from cramped silences;

a steamed up kitchen where sleeves swipe glass
to see if clouds cataract the sky.
We wipe mirrors too, free fogged reflections
again – and yet again.
All surfaces we keep clear except for one
milk white orb father has for sight
leaving him straining for vision, us
grown smaller than the words
blown up under his magnifying moon
tracking pages in newspapers
spread wide like the heavens.

Leviathan,
our wagon train where we shoot each other down
pretending to be dead, getting up again –
and yet again;

you have pierced dark places,
beamed star clusters bright as joy
those windfall days we found
galaxies beyond our own.

Returning home with as much fruit
as we could carry, bitter sweetness
burrowed under thin membranes
broken already by birds

later cored to empty sockets
shaped like stars.

I fill today
with as much remembered light
as I can bear.

My Dress Hangs There
(After a painting by Frida Kahlo)

What's left of it is draped across
the remains of buildings levelled to the ground
or floating under skies smuggled away by flame.

What use is it here? What business
an old dress, out of fashion
losing its shape
fluttering from these rooms
an apartment block six floors up?

If my children ever ask,
I will show them what I took from it
tied up with string in a battered suitcase
hidden at the back of the wardrobe:

some buttons glazed with tears, shed
by my mother, my sister;
sieving fool's gold, pinpricks of daylight
through a cellar window;
a collar drenched in my father's blood and sweat.

From its torn-off pocket I'll shake out
sounds of shells, heavy footsteps in the night,
sirens calling.
My dress hangs in that place, still on parade.
So thin it is become
moonlight slices through. For this

would my children exchange the food in their bellies
the shoes on their feet, the clothes on their backs?

Strawberry Thief

It's dawn at Kelmscott.
Nature tumbles from tree and vine;
flits of shadow over summer's loom
weave a trellis of light.

Tousle-haired, unshaven,
driven from sleep by heaviness of shape
not yet defined, William Morris stares
at strays of colour
rambling just beyond his vision.
A mistle thrush swoops to feast,
spears with beak
through to the centre of the fruit

the way a needle pierces cloth.

Glossed with dew, leaves sway
to the rhythm of the bird's
unceasing labour. The housekeeper
moves to stop the plunder;

indignation is stayed
by a hand well used
to weft and warp of fabric.

In the middle of his purpose
the mistle thrush breaks into song,
sings his joy
with each full-throated note.

A skyward soar,
patterns swirls of flight
washes the cotton of feather
indigo.

Mr Einstein

You make unsettled days easier to bear.
Days, pre-ordained as a migrant's journey,
like swallows from my clothesline.

Thank you for your parallel worlds
where past, future, wretched in-betweens
nappies, work-shirts, age-bleached dresses,
make a place for me –

nights new as stars –

I swirled home from dances
with shocks of kissing on my lips;

to still exist in some other space
on these unsettled days of swallows,
pegging down the ordinary.

For Emily

I can still see those rows of blue,
these young women; apple-cheeked
plump in gymslip pleats.

That brown schoolroom. Ms. Hogan,
this passionate odyssey clasped
in her white hands. Heathcliff,

dark love that took me
beyond drizzled windows.
Fifteen, barely a woman,

yet there were nights when I re-wrote
whole passages until fictions merged
with fact, became the shock of morning;

faded walls, worn lino, cold to the first bare touch,
downstairs father's wheezy cough,
sounds of mother coaxing the Aga's warmth.

Somewhere between wild moors,
my own perimeter, I found
an ageless presence:

though I barter imagined kisses
for the scent and taste of flesh.

Firebirds

One of them had a missing front tooth.
Her smile was like a slightly parted door
opened wide in her bedroom at night;
no-one to see or hear howling wind
or river rushing underneath the bridge
the shop was built on.

Her hair was a thin tissue of soft brown
powdered by soot. She was somehow
connected to the older woman
who owned the shop, smelling of coal
and baby powders (I liked that smell)
whose snow coloured web of hair

shocked the blue of her eyes.

Trapped under a hairnet, beads
of tiny pearls glowed, a nest of embers
glimpsed from the leaded fireplace
in the kitchen just beyond
jelly jars, fat marshmallows.

Coal dust hung over everything as
a line of crows might settle on
aluminium tins and canisters. Always
there was the smell of soot on wine gums,
liquorice allsorts.

In a dream I bought a bag of apples there,
gilded as if some sorcery feathered
over them. I bit into fermented fruit
and firebirds, two of them,

flew around my mouth, down
the back of my throat, down into
the black stove of my belly
lighting to a roaring furnace, fires
I could not, would not, put out.

Not then.

Star-splitters
(For Adrian)
After 'The Star-splitter' by Robert Frost

Brad McLaughlin burnt down his house,
blackened the green skin of his fields
and, with insurance, bought himself a telescope.
A fair exchange it was, stones for stars.
I know a man like this, a man
whose place is in the doing not the saying,
though he had no farm to set in flames, who
'beyond the age of being given one
for Christmas gift'
took the best way he knew how
to find himself in one.
To know where he stood exactly
when it comes to splitting stars
or splitting hairs or anything else
for that matter.
And so,
he took the white sky of his arm,
inked blues and reds the whole
celestial length of it;
smoky lanterns
of a longing often doused
by daylight hours.
He charts his own Orion, a telescope
in which to find himself.
Just as black, just as velvety
as Brad McLaughlin's who incidentally said
'Someone in every town
seems to me owes it to the town to keep one.
In Littleton, it might as well be me.'

Vodka Light

pierces through mornings
memory cannot wipe clean
of mornings, so many
uncapped
poured
into burning spaces
set ablaze by vodka fires.

Vodka light is drenched
in vodka smell, swallow-

fulls of bitter words
doused in blind light.

Shadow shaping words
sift their way back
through
shades of vodka
coloured light;

smudged this morning
on windows
memory
cannot
wipe
clean.

Fire Fox

When the arctic fox sweeps his tail
along packed tight snow, powdering
crystals rise to meet the sun. Stirred up
by solar winds this dust returns,
showering a flail of light to startle
Northern skies.

So folklore tells it.

One day, a mirror slips from my hands,
slivers into tiny cracks scarce held together
in a compact case. Shards fan out
a sheaf of superstition. Seven years' wilderness

maybe seven more divining skitters of life
breathing beneath the ice.

I think how that wild fox roams
a stilled white landscape
invisible in his blending coat
yet each movement detonates fires.
A thaw of possibility dips my brush
in fiery coals, paints broken particles

blue, green and orange burnings
that flare from the frozen page

send back flame.

Kestrel at Tymon Park

This bird, though small — her wimpling wings
would scarce fill my outstretched hand from fingertip
to wrist —

is large enough to be the female of her breed;
firing powerful engines that breathe like mysteries
through the rise and fall of centuries.

Empress of the skies, her pin eye
is trained on bustling grasses, alive with insects
fattening her breast — attracting the mate
who must surely clade with her here
on this green heath, find his own hovering height
over a lake succulent with frog, blue damsel fly.
She is no fool, her beak was blooded in places such as
this,

while sleeping earth was forced to yield
she soared; oblivious to decades of change,
traffic snarling past these iron gates.
Her eye can penetrate densest marl
the way filtering light through thinning branches,
sycamore, alder, beech
lures down to brute earth skin on skin,
scents of hurried love faltering
into history. This is not her story.

She bides her time, can live in nests
vacated by other birds. She can rise
high as sixty feet, far higher than anything else
stroking Tallaght landscape. High over
streams of creed and colour unspooled

across Sunday walkways, skimming
coppiced woodlands, heavy hedgerows,
feasts of elderberries. Fruits she has no taste for.
Up she soars, taking me with her
up up
until I can go no further, falling back
on the words of a poem that fly into my mouth
from an old forgotten place. She grows smaller,
becomes a speck to my human eye,
but my heart swells,
is stirred by such a bird as she;

> *Oh, the achieve of*
> *the mastery of the thing.*

The Man With Scythes for Arms

He swishes through the kitchen,
black dark outside, midnight in the cupboards.

Who knows what's in his head,

what shape or sense he sees
around the chairs; cushions plump
as the breasts of the woman
he is harnessed to, her belly
protruding under him.

He rides the night ride up those stairs
awkward like a colt trying to stand.
There he'll lie until the woman on his back,

the woman who looks as if she has just
plopped out of a large pink jelly mould

pulls away from him. Joined at the hip for now
by his dead end job
her lack of somewhere else to go.

What he sees in the morning as he sways tall,
hollyhock tall, hairy, forgotten to shave
what he sees is the swell of his brood
squeezed into corners

his swishing cannot reach
though today his blades are blunt
and the grass, though overgrown,
holds no threat for now.

In a trick of half-light
he catches sight of his shadow
scythes for arms
hooves for feet.

An Fear Gorm

A black rink covers the schoolroom wall,
scratched from chalk skated over it. One slip
brings the smell of leather, stripes hands
the way liquorice blackens the tongue.
Black is heard too. In boots lurching up the street
towards black-in-the-face waiting women,
in whispers of night time rosaries, fingers weaving
prayer through black beads.

In this world of black, An Fear Gorm
is the blue flame over Kitty Seery's seal-shiny hair,
river-blue veins in atlases, the faint ridge
around grandmother's wedding china.
His skin is the cool breeze of blue ice-cream
pictured in magazines, cut out and pasted
into scrapbooks beside blue high heels
the exact shades of blueberry pie.
An Fear Gorm fills the dusty inkwells,
dry as African plains,
with enough blue to spill across white pages.

In this world of black,
our native language colours the black man blue,
as if our forebears couldn't believe he ever existed,
as if a blue man is rare as a blue moon
in a pitch black sky.

Hummingbird and Owl

This well is an orchid
struggling green shoots skywards.

Sympodial;
sending out tiger spotted trails, new leads
leaving roots for dead, saving some back
for dry seasons.

The hummingbird's long bill is a diviner's rod
pulling this way and that,

diving such frenzies down
an orchid's throat,

drilling through purples, pinks,
blazing reds

drawing them up to hovering tongue tip,

sucking the juice from them.

This well, midnight inked, swallows
whole the landscape.
An incandescent moon
flickers between the skins of two worlds;

memory maps break bindings.

Here the owl with night vision, talons extended,
seeks and finds the heft and cleave of prey;

steadies a line of wing
drinking the colour blue.

Photographs of a Girl

Black and white pleats bunch on the woodpile,
thighs a peek-a-boo flash of pale as cotton
summer. Her doll face is streaked by streels
of doll fine hair. Doll small hands plait together.
She stares out over a garden with sweet
un-expected scents as if some hidden camera
is just about to explode.

(ii)

Under a table she slides, like some anonymous
envelope.
On her jacket, eagle-wide wings feather down her
sleeve
shadow-long trousers crease a knife-edge.
Screened off, a piano is pricked with studs of light,
lid closed tight.

(iii)

Behind ropes of hair, her face splits into shards:
nose, mouth, eyes. Freckles shiver on November skin.
In her hand, a full purse is held with a two-fingered
grip.
Shoulder blades jagger out of a short sleeved tee-shirt.
The angle of an elbow bundles up what's left of her
from the waist down, on this windswept day
as she perches over a railing
her smile in ruins.

(iv)

She is a tangled weave of geometry,
circles under her eyes, hair cut to points,
nose sloping down to flat-lined mouth.
Her neck is collared in wisps of braided hair,
pearls of globular blue streaked under
fine eyebrows. Web thin skeins of veins
bruise their silkworm path under her skin.

(v)

Her mouth parts slightly, hair pinned back,
chin shadow is a stain on the white of her neck
child-like yet old as the shapes that rise
behind the house where she once lived.
Tiny lines furrow the brow, tiny creases
fold like a taffeta gown.

(vi)

In the circle of her shoulder, the last bit of sun
pierces down. For the seconds it takes
to take this photograph
she wears a red dress, makes a red dive
with outstretched arms
to colour the pavement red, like a shark
that's just had its throat cut.

Her eyes are clearings with blue lakes
Her forehead is a desert
Her hair is a tangle of night
Her mouth is an ocean
Red silk flowers

Her face
Is the face
Of a child

Novenas

Prayer will pull her through. So she's been told
by the well meaning who don't like to interfere
the ones who barely speak to her unless trouble
is at the door.

Prayer will pull her through;

two funerals in one year
her eldest beaten up
the knocks her husband gives her,
whether in or out of humour.
Now this latest blow, the baby's vacant stare
gets her up in the small hours
when the house is quiet.

Her novenas, forty a day, un-tipped,
are kept safe behind the mantle clock
or tucked inside a handbag.
She lights her thin white candle

swallows deep the first prayer of the day.
It pulls her through,

great lungfuls of it.

Warriors

The Grand Canal is silvery as a new coin.
I'm on the Luas thinking of nothing in particular
when a man, swift as an antelope,
runs from the houses towards Suir Road.

Legs, long as spears, gather speed.
This Luas is a wild one

broken free from the herd.

On the grass, thawing frost steams a mirage,
dust rises.
His winter coat, shirt and navy trousers
dissolve to gorgeous Masai colours.
He gleams like the skin on these tracks,
each muscle and sinew
zig zagging a perfect quarter arc

bearing down on the metal beast,
and I'm back on the Midland streets

side-stepping pools of greenish-
hued cow dung. Straw
straggles from trailers, haggling
wasps swarm around my ears.

A cow breaks from a loose bunch
is chased by a farmer in breeches
held up with braces, his face berry red,
legs akimbo; the stick in his hand
orchestrating a fair day.
Later, there'll be whiskey in the pubs

chocolate for children of the tribe
creeping in to sit on the long benches.

My warrior comes on board
scarcely out of breath. Beyond

Rialto
Fatima
St. James's
Heuston Station

we journey towards the city.

Woman in a White Headscarf

Pale as cloud is the moon shape of her face
circled by the silk of her scarf.
Dressed full length in black coat, boots,
flat lace-ups, her hands are small pink peeps
holding tight to a wheelbarrow
pitted over stone trundled earth
covered full length in mud.

Shadows of soldiers with rifles
cut across shadows struggling to rebuild.

At nightfall in this captive city
a woman flutters down her spine
the white flag of the day's surrender,
releases to black

the birds of her hair.

Gold
(For Ann Marie Mullen)

Pulled after me, this shopping trolley

could just as easily be a fur-packed sleigh
or the timber-laden bogey
father brought from the saw-mill.

Perched on a dustbin, a heron rises,

kicks back its legs for take-off;

a windblown umbrella
sailing over roof-tops white with frost.

At Sean Walsh Park
shadows break at the railings
for this middle-aged Magus and her gift.
I pause for breath

give praise to Raphael, Angel of Divine Love.

For you, Ann Marie,

I would pull this trolley with Christmas tree
up the Himalayas. Over the bridge at least
leading to the shopping centre –
even if it crossed the snapping jaws of crocodiles –

to come to our Thursday space;

unfold for you
branch and leaf

plug this tree into the mains
the way an engine on a frozen morning
must be coaxed to full throttle,
or
how a fractured heart
barely ticking over is soldered
by your Midas hands

showering a hail of

Sun
Moon
Stars

Cinema Paradiso
(For Dwain and Naomi)

Already older, you are gone on
ahead of time and date
documenting this recording
we squash around the t.v. set to watch
in this room full of collective clutter;

books, more books, computer stuff
and a musty piano with missing keys.

You will always be twenty-two weeks old
in this fifteen-minute ultrasound screening
perfectly at ease in your mother's womb,
everything as it should be
on this Master copy; living proof

you will not come into the world as
your grandmother did,

a puzzle in a pleated skirt
hair parted, head to one side
like a bird listening out for
your great-grandmother's voice
or the creak of the garden gate
being lifted up, rushed forward

all of what went before
the age of three. Gone fuzzy
like a bad bootleg version.

I imagine you grown up
seeing yourself like this

filling in the best bits as I am
wide-eyed at this sight of you,
everything as it should be;

the great big heart of the universe
beating
no matter what.

Song

'A bird doesn't sing because it has an answer
It sings because it has a song' — Maya Angelou

Wet that first soaring note on your tongue,
  thread it through morning's needle,
    sewing as much as can be spared
      into your spending purse.

Slather it under a vest —
  it's a lot warmer
    than Eskimo grease.

Brush teeth with it too,
  throw back your head,
    gargle an aria.

Smather it over hands,
  inhale as if taking in
    snuff at a wedding.

Store a scoop or two of it
  hollowed deep in skin
    it will be there —
      when it's most needed.

Don't leave it padlocked
  to the railings
    or smothered
      in the boot of a car.

Taste cello or saxophone
each passing hour
bite on every chord

let it rush headlong
into your belly

climb after it;

no fool's gold, this.

Derelict

So much depends upon a blue building
two white letters, like two front teeth,
missing from its name; gashes of light
seeped through boarded up windows.

So much depends upon its flitters of paint
stripping down to a flimsy blue dress
worn by a girl with seams in her stockings,
borrowed lipstick bruised over her mouth.

So much depends on the boy
cycling hard against the wind,
coming breathless to where she waits
his skin sandpapery with stubble;

so much depending on the cinema
becoming the hardware store,
yard brushes stiff as the back of a porcupine,
stainless steel glints on scrubbed floorboards.

So much depends on a blue building,
a totem grazed by autumn
towering over parked cars

people going about their business.

Crane

High enough for a Stylite's
Alice in Wonderland
Experience
Above ants
Hoarding from Marks
& Spencer's
Or
Captain Americas.
Not so high
Smells of
Kick-ass
Food
Can't tempt
Those forty
Days and nights.

Narrow enough
So a tightrope walker
From
Azerbaijan
Can high-wire
Across Niagara skyline
As he did
One summer here
So long ago;
A memory
Ratcheted
On this
Long legged
Yellow
Metal
Bird.

Man at Sea

Churls of memory, mightier than anything
ploughing the waves, hurl themselves up
rising and rinsing silver, lizard faces
treacherous as betrayal.

This drunken trawler lurches its midnight sprawl,
a man could be lost in this brawl of spray.
All night the skin of this ocean breaks,
unleashes dragons that ride alongside
dousing old wood with unfathomable depths.
Below deck, pots and pans prattle out reminders;

slide into view another place and time;
a woman's skin, warm in lamplight,
her hair slithering like uncoiled snakes
down her naked back.

No matter how long at sea
the body never forgets the ravages of passion,
or how a sliver of steel glints a silhouette
reflected in a puddle of rain outside
the Church of Broken Promises.

Missing

So someone might remember, piece together
hours that lit her presence; in a paragraph
she breathes.

Months dim the weeks dimming
the days. Her face strays out of focus,
colours of her bright anorak
blur into yesterday's news.

Every now and then a headline or a photograph
moves her large as life in slow motion
like the little girl in a red coat
Schindler stared at when he gazed upon
sepia crowds filing past his window.

Brown Bird Bottle

A bird with an eye span
round as the rim of a brown bottle
long crouched in sleep
at the back of my tongue

wakes in a flap of feathery sails.

Silk to taste for all their senseless flight.

A brown bird swoops
through that thin tunnel of breath
down to the nesting pit
where many the fledgling hour
was pushed off the edge
of that steep cliff.
Whole days lost
like a shipwrecked crew
tossed on the rocks below.

A bead-eyed bird preens itself,
waits for the wind to rise,
for sightings of a reckless flag
hoisted to the lips of morning.
These sea changes do not come.

A brown bird
whose sailing feathers are sleek
as glass glinted in sunlight
pours out the last sour drop
of a song I am no longer
eager to hear or fill my throat
or belly with.

I open the door of its cage

and let it go.

Wish

If I am to be visited
let that being be part female,
green, full, all shades of it,
so my heart can heal.
Part male, with a violet aura
spreading towards the edges
so I can forgive,
be forgiven.

Let that being
have the face of my child
pressing against the glass,
looking in
meeting my eyes
so I know
it is my child come home.

Don't let me be blinded
by false energy or light;
let me be fully alert
with all my pores open
ready to receive
whatever small bounty
this being might bring.